wicked
FRENCH

BY HOWARD TOMB

D0012625

WORKMAN PUBLISHING · NEW YORK

ACKNOWLEDGMENTS
Many thanks to Elizabeth Rivière, Gabriel Landau,
Sophie Gillet, Christine Ruggeri, Michael Cader, Sally
Kovalchick, Carol McKeown, Patty Brown, John
Boswell, Renée Lowther, and Ben Stoner.

Library of Congress Cataloging-in-Publication Data
Tomb, Howard, 1959–
  Wicked French.

  1. French language—Conversation and phrase
books—Humor. 2. France—Description and
travel—1975—Guide-books—Humor. 3. Voyages and
travels—Humor. I. Title.
PN6231.F745T66 1989   448.3'421'0207   88-40229
ISBN 0-89480-616-5

Illustrations by Jared Lee
Cover and book design by Paul Hanson

Workman Publishing Company, Inc.
708 Broadway
New York, NY 10003

Manufactured in the United States of America
First printing June 1989

10 9 8 7 6 5 4 3 2 1

CONTENTS

BUREAUCRACY AND CULTURE

WINE AND FOOD

CAFE AND NIGHTLIFE

THE MODEL GUEST

WELCOME TO FRANCE

French people believe that they invented Western civilization. In fact, many of them doubt that cultural refinement has ever spread beyond the borders of their *beau pays*.

They may be right, but that's no reason to be intimidated by everyone and everything French. We do not have to feel inferior to French toddlers, French pig farmers, or French cats and dogs, for example.

Granted, they all may be able to tell a Burgundy from a Bordeaux. They may have a firm grasp of the subjunctive tense. They may know Jacques Cousteau personally. But we play better basketball. Our mountains are bigger than theirs. And we saved them from the Germans.

This book is intended to help transform readers into complete travelers, capable of subtle understanding, intelligent discourse, and effective verbal assault.

Bonne chance.

MAKING FRENCH NOISES WITH YOUR MOUTH AND NOSE

Americans find French accents charming. This is because they imagine that French people are so-phisticated and intelligent.

The French find the accents of Americans speaking French nauseating. This is because they imagine that Americans are boorish and stupid.

A traveler in France may wish to obtain such things as a hotel room, a bottle of beer, or a ticket home. Without the proper accent, such luxuries may not be forthcoming. Frenchmen will feel free

THE UNTRANSLATABLES

The following phrases have no meaning in France. Do not make an attempt to translate them.

French fries	French Canadian
French bread	French dressing
French pastry	French toast
French cuffs	French leave
French kissing	French doors
French dry cleaning	French windows
French heels	French horn
French restaurant	French poodle
	French letter

to torment you. They may never reveal that they speak English perfectly.

Many of the sounds made by French people are never made by English-speaking mouths. These peculiar noises are therefore difficult to describe and to imitate. Nevertheless, you must attempt to approximate a French accent if you hope to avoid being seen as a creature totally unworthy of respect, *un boucher de la langue sacrée* (a butcher of the holy tongue).

The *U* in *STUPIDE*

The *u* in *stupide* is a tough one, but learning it is crucial. Without it, you will be unable to say such things as:

These stinking truffles are overrated.	*Ces truffes puantes sont surfaites.*	*Say trÿf pÿ-ONT sohn SŸR-fet.*
Stop at my petticoat, Luc, you beastly peasant!	*Ne te rue pas sur mon jupon, Luc, espèce de rustaud brutal!*	*Nuh tuh rÿ pah sÿr mohn jÿ-POHN, Lÿk, esspess duh RŸS-toh brÿ-TAHL!*
This nectarine is very tough.	*Ce brugnon est très dur.*	*Suh brÿn-YON ay tray dÿr.*

Making the sound requires holding the lips out in an O shape, imitating the look of interest sometimes seen on the faces of chimpanzees, while making the sound "eee." It does *not* sound like "ooo." The sound, to our ears, suggests sharp disgust.

The *u* in *stupide* will be designated in the phonetic instructions as *ÿ*.

The *R* in *RUDE*

The flat *r* Americans use is painful to Continental ears. Some French *r*'s are silent, as in the verb *aimer*, to love, which is pronounced "AY-may." *R*'s that are pronounced are rolling and guttural, as in "Grrruffles have grrridges."

Practice with the following phrases:

I prefer drinking battery acid to reading Rimbaud.	*Je préfère boire l'acide d'une batterie de voiture que lire du Rimbaud.*	*Shuh pray-FARE bwarr LAH-seed dÿn bat-ree duh vwah-TŸR kuh leer dÿ ram-BOH.*
The repulsive Citroën burps and bellows like a rhinoceros.	*La Citroën rébarbative rote et rugit comme un rhinocéros.*	*Lah SEE-troh-en ray-BAR-bah-TEEV rote ay rÿ-JEE cum uhn REE-noh-sair-OSS.*
Okay, Pierre, but be careful not to spoil my hairdo.	*D'accord, Pierre, mais garde-toi d'ébouriffer ma coiffure.*	*DAK-or, Pyair, may GAR-duh-twah DAY-boor-ee-FAY mah kwah-FŸR.*

The *N* in *RIEN*

The French sound for *n* invariably issues from the sinuses. It can be pronounced perfectly well with the mouth closed.

PRONUNCIATION DISCLAIMER

Subtleties of pronunciation must be learned by listening. No book, no matter how cunning or imaginative it may be, can quite describe the sounds made by French people.

The author and publisher take no responsibility for errors of pronunciation that result in one or more of the following: any *faux pas* or *gaffe*; the offense of any host or other native; the regrettable consumption of any food or food-like substance; arrival at any (wrong) place at any (wrong) time; or any and all of the tragedies, calamities, inconveniences, and embarrassments traditionally experienced by tone-deaf tourists the world over.

FRIENDLY CUSTOMS AGENTS AND THEIR MACHINE GUNS

Because of the behavior of certain ruffians and scoundrels, security is tighter than ever at French ports of entry. In evidence at airports are boys who wear bullet-proof vests, tote real machine guns, and whisper commands to their large dogs. The agents and soldiers ignore almost everyone, but woe to the one who attracts their attention.

I'm here for pleasure/ business.	*Je suis ici pour le plaisir/les affaires.*	*Shuh sweez ee-see poor luh play-ZEER/laze ah-FAIR.*
I have nothing to declare.	*Je n'ai rien à déclarer.*	*Shuh nay ĸYEN ah DAY-clah-RAY.*
Must you open the bags?	*Devez-vous ouvrir les bagages?*	*DUH-vay-voo oo-vreer lay bah-GAHJ?*
Nice doggie!	*Oh le beau toutou!*	*Oh luh boh too-TOO!*
Of course, you're welcome to tear my suitcase apart.	*Bien sûr, soyez le bienvenu pour réduire ma valise en miettes.*	*Byen SŸR, swah-yay luh byen-ven-ÿ poor ray-dweer mah vah-LEEZ on MYET.*

Lucky they're only these tacky Louis Vuitton bags!	*Heureusement ce ne sont que des valises moches de Louis Vuitton!*	*UR-uz-mon suh nuh sohn kuh day vah-leez mosh duh Loo-ee Vwee-TON!*
No, I didn't pack any Roquefort.	*Non, je n'ai pas de Roquefort.*	*Nohn, shuh nay PAH duh Roh-keh-FOR.*
I think you smell my socks.	*Je pense que ce sont mes chaussettes que vous reniflez.*	*Shuh PONCE kuh suh sohn may shoh-SET kuh voo ron-ee-flay.*

PRAYER OF THE FREQUENT FLIER

O Saint Mercury, Mighty Messenger, Lord of Speed, deliver us to the airport on time. Our tickets are nonrefundable, Your Heavenly Rapidity. I swear I had no idea traffic would be so bad, Your Swiftness.

Saint-Mercure, Messager Puissant, Seigneur Incontesté de la Vélocité, déposez-nous à temps à notre aéroport. Nos billets ne sont plus valides après ce soir. Je vous jure, o Saint Patron de la Rapidité, que je n'avais aucune idée des embouteillages avec lesquels nous serions confrontés.

GETTING AROUND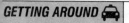

TAXI DRIVER

Your life is in his hands. Your heart is in your throat. Isn't Paris exciting? Don't you wish you'd worn diapers?

Most Parisian taxi drivers are not homicidal; they are simply bored. Their own need for adrenaline usually outweighs their concern for their customers' health and happiness.

Whenever you encounter a taxi driver alone, feel free to remind him that he is your servant.

Turn right/left.	*Tournez à droite/ gauche.*	TOUR-nay ah dwot/goash.
Where did you learn to drive? Italy?	*Où avez-vous appris à conduire? En Italie?*	OO ah-vay voo ah-pree ah con-DWEER? On ee-tal-EE?
Slow down or die.	*Moins vite, ou crève.*	Mwann VEET, oo krev.

🚕 **GETTING AROUND**

You missed the turn, imbecile!	*Vous avez manqué la rue, imbécile!*	*Vooz ah-vay mahn-kay lah RŸ, ahm-bay-SEEL!*
Stop here.	*Arrêtez-vous ici.*	*Ah-ret-ay voo ee-SEE.*
I'll pay only what's on the meter, you idiot.	*Je ne payerai que le prix indiqué sur le compteur, espèce d'idiot.*	*Shuh nuh pay-er-ay kuh luh pree an-dee-KAY sÿr luh com-TURR, ess-pess dee-DYOH.*
Do you take me for a fool?	*Vous me prenez pour un clown?*	*Voo muh pruh-nay poor uhn CLOON?*
Don't you know who I am, you numbskull?	*Savez-vous qui je suis, cervelle d'oiseau?*	*Sav-ay VOO kee shuh SWEE, sair-VEL dwah-ZOH?*
Oh yeah? Your wife says the same thing about you!	*Ah oui? Votre femme disait la même chose de vous!*	*Ah WEE? Voh-truh FAHM dee-zay lah mem shows duh VOO!*

GETTING AROUND 🚕

TAXI DRIVER *AVEC* CUJO

Parisian drivers are horrifying enough armed only with a car, but some cabs are also equipped with vicious *chiens*. Do not be taken in by small size and an adorable haircut; when such a beast is present, the driver must be treated gingerly. Verbal attacks should be subtle or ambiguous.

Drop us off anywhere you like.	*Déposez-nous où vous voulez.*	*DAY-poh-zay NOO ooh voo VOO-lay.*
Take any route you wish.	*Prenez la route que vous préfèrez.*	*PREN-ay lah ROOT kuh voo PRAY-fair-AY.*
I was sure you would kill those pedestrians.	*Je savais bien que vous alliez écraser ces piétons.*	*Shuh sav-ay BYEN kuh vooz al-yay AY-crah-zay say pyay-TOHN.*
You are a superb driver.	*Vous êtes un as du volant.*	*Voo-zet uhn NAHSS dÿ voh-lon.*
Have you ever considered a career in auto racing?	*Vous n'avez jamais pensé à une carrière de coureur automobile?*	*Voo nah-vay SHAM-ay ponce-ay ah ÿn cah-ree-YAIR duh coo-RUR oh-toh-moh-BEEL?*

What a beautiful poodle you have.	*Quel beau caniche vous avez là.*	*Kell boh can-EESH vooz ah-vay lah.*
I adore fat, cross-eyed dogs.	*Je raffole des gros chiens qui louchent.*	*Shuh rah-FOHL day grow shee-YEN kee LOOSH.*
Eight thousand francs?	*Huit mille francs?*	*Wee meel fron?*
That sounds reasonable.	*Cela semble raisonnable.*	*Suh-lah SOM-bluh RAY-zoh-nah-bluh.*
Of course, It means our vacation will end today.	*Bien sûr, cela veut dire que nos vacances se terminent aujourd'hui.*	*Byen SŸR, suh-lah vuh deer kuh noh vah-CONCE suh tare-MEEN oh-shore-DWEE.*
It was an honor to ride in your excellent taxi.	*Ce fut un honneur de rouler dans votre excellent taxi.*	*Suh fÿt uh non-UR duh roo-lay dahn voh-truh EX-ell-ahn tack-SEE.*

KILOMETERS PER HOUR: GET A GRIP

Gas is so expensive in France that almost everyone has to drive wimpy little cars. This makes motorists feel impotent. They compensate by driving at what are literally breakneck speeds. The preferred highway cruising speed is 215 kilometers per hour (kph), or 133 mph.

Travelers who plan to get behind the wheel should first familiarize themselves with kph and how speed limits apply to various situations.

FRENCH ROAD SIGN   TRANSLATIONS

	ENGLISH	KPH	MPH
Stop	**Stop**	60	35
École	**School Zone**	80	50
Chantier	**Men Working**	150	95
Virages Dangereux	**Hairpin Turns**	175	110
Cochon: Attention	**Truffle Pig Crossing**	200	125
Mouton: Attention	**Sheep Crossing**	225	140
Prière d'Attacher la Ceinture de Sécurité	**Fasten Seat Belt**	250	155
Porsche Devant	**Porsche Ahead**	275	170

RONDPOINT TECHNIQUE AND RECOMMENDED ARMAMENTS

Because the French dislike large intersections, they have developed an alternative: *rondpoints* (roundabouts). This is the Continental form of stock car racing.

Once inside the circle, you will find yourself hemmed in by hundreds of tiny, careening cars. Packing a picnic may be a good idea for long afternoons in the *rondpoint*. Remember: food may be *projeté* (tossed about) inside your vehicle. Avoid fondue dishes.

Sturdy helmets and flameproof suits are helpful. Large-bore pistols, automatic assault rifles, and flame throwers may come in handy when you're ready to clear a path to an exit.

EPITHETS ON WHEELS

Shouting at French drivers in English is profoundly unsatisfying. To elicit expressions of shock and embarrassment from driving opponents, you must communicate with them in their own language.

Hey! Get a license, grandpa!	*Hé! Va apprendre à conduire, pépé!*	*AY! Vah ah-PRAWN-druh ah con-DWEER, pay-pay!*
Move that worthless heap off the road!	*Ôte ce tas de férraille de la circulation!*	*Ote suh tah duh fair-EYE duh lah SEER-kÿ-lass yon!*
Which are you? Blind? Or blind drunk?	*Quoi? T'es aveugle? Ou complètement bourré?*	*Kwah? Tay ah-VUH-gluh? Oo com-plett-mahn boo-RAY?*
Open your eyes, imbecile!	*Ouvre les yeux, imbécile!*	*OO-vruh lay-ZYUH, am-bay-SEEL!*
Get off my tail, garlic head!	*Cesse de me filer le train, tronche d'aïl!*	*Sess duh muh fee-lay luh TRAN, tronsh dah-YEE!*
Your mother is Belgian!	*Ta mère est belge!*	*Tah mare ay BELJH!*

LESSER-KNOWN INTERNATIONAL SYMBOLS

All motorists must learn to decipher basic road signs. But there are many obscure international symbols that alert the astute driver to cultural hazards and opportunities.

RUDE
SHOPKEEPERS
NEXT 15 KM

SMELLY
FISHERMEN
SMOKING
GAULOISES

NO BERETS

WARNING:
BAD MIME
AHEAD

YET ANOTHER
MATISSE MUSEUM
1 KM

FINE POINTS OF THE PARIS METRO

On the Paris Métro, certain seats are reserved for war veterans, pregnant women, and so on. These seats are marked for *les anciens combattants.*

When there are too many mothers-to-be and veterans for the number of special seats, a complex system goes into effect. Riders with the fewest remaining limbs get priority. If two veterans have the same number of limbs, World War I veterans are seated before those of World War II. Members of the French Résistance win two seats if Charles de Gaulle ever kissed them.

For those who must have a seat at any cost, a few plausible lines are provided.

I was in the Résistance.	*J'étais dans la Résistance.*	*SHAY-tay dahn lah RAY-zees-tonce.*
As an infant.	*Comme nourrisson.*	*CUM noo-ree-SOHN.*
I carried messages in my diapers.	*Je transportais des messages dans mes langes.*	*Shuh TRAHN-spoor-tay day MAY-sahj dahn may LOHN-juh.*
No one dared to search them.	*Personne n'a jamais osé les fouiller.*	*PAIR-sun nah SHAH-may oh-zay lay FOO-yay.*

🚗 **GETTING AROUND**

But a swine informer turned me in.	*Mais un salopard d'indicateur m'a dénoncé.*	*May uhn SAL-oh-parr DAN-dee-cah-turr mah DAY-nohn-say.*
I was tortured by the Gestapo.	*J'ai été torturé par la Gestapo.*	*Shay ay-tay TORE-tÿ-ray par lah GAY-stop-oh.*
I told them nothing.	*Je ne leur ai rien dit.*	*Shuh nuh lurr ay RYEN dee.*
I escaped in the bathwater.	*Je me suis échappé par l'écoulement de la baignoire.*	*Shuh muh swee ZAY-sha-pay par lay-cool-MOHN duh lah ben-warr.*
Give me that seat.	*Cédez-moi votre siège.*	*SAY-day-mwah voh-truh see-YEHJ.*

RAILWAY ROMANCE

French trains are among the best in the world, but they aren't perfect; one is obliged to share them with the French. Newer trains like the Très Grande Vitesse (TGV, or "Really Big Speed") have an open seating plan, but some of the older trains are still on the tracks. Their cars are divided into compartments that seat six people each.

As every sophisticated traveler knows, there is nothing like a special moment alone with a loved one in a speeding train. The rocking motion of the car, the long, dark tunnels, and the possibility of arrest create an irresistibly romantic atmosphere. The following phrases are meant to help lovers win the private compartment they need to make their train ride really memorable.

Excuse me.	*Excusez-moi.*	*Ex-KŸ-zay mwah.*
Would you mind clipping my toenails?	*Cela vous ennuyerait de me couper les ongles des orteils?*	*Suh-lah voo zon-nwee-RAY duh muh coo-pay lay ZON-gluh day-zor-TAY?*
Whoops! Sorry! I didn't mean to spill that coffee on you.	*Oh! Pardon! Je n'ai pas fait exprès de vous renverser mon café dessus.*	*Oh! PAR-dohn! Shuh nay pah fay ex-PRAY duh voo RON-vair-say mohn caf-ay deh-SŸ.*

I really like your moustache.	*J'aime beaucoup votre moustache.*	*Shem BOH-coo voh-truh moo-STASH.*
It's charming on an older woman.	*C'est charmant sur une vieille dame.*	*Say shar-MAHN sÿr ÿn vyay dahm.*
You must have been beautiful when you were young.	*Vous deviez être très belle quand vous étiez jeune.*	*Voo DUH-vyay et-ruh TRAY bell con voo zay-tyay juhn.*
But those front teeth of yours look dead.	*Mais vos dents de devant ont l'air fichues.*	*May voh DON duh duh-VON on lair FEE-shÿ.*

ACCOMMODATIONS

NOTORIOUS SNOUTS, PART I: THE CONCIERGE

Should you rent an apartment in France, your concierge may be a woman who finds her excitement in the intimate details of her tenants' lives. It's best to set the record straight at the beginning.

No, we aren't married.	*Non, nous ne sommes pas mariés.*	*NOHN, noo nuh somm PAH mah-ree-ay.*
This is my niece/cousin/ daughter/ granddaughter.	*C'est ma nièce/ cousine/fille/ petite-fille.*	*Say mah nee-YES/coo-ZEEN/ FEE/puh-TEET fee.*
No, my wife will not be joining us.	*Non, ma femme ne viendra pas nous rejoindre.*	*NOHN, mah fahm nuh vyen-drah PAH noo ruh-JWAN-druh.*
Yes, she knows we are here.	*Oui, elle sait que nous sommes ici.*	*WEE, ell say kuh noo sum zee-SEE.*
No, there is no need for you to telephone her.	*Non, vous n'avez pas besoin de lui téléphoner.*	*NOHN, voo nah-vay PAH buzz-wan duh lwee TAY-lay-fone-AY.*

ACCOMMODATIONS

NOTORIOUS SNOUTS, PART II: THE *RECEPTIONISTE*

The female traveler should be aware that the male *réceptioniste* found at a hotel has just two goals in life: making your stay more comfortable, and getting a date. He whimpers and pleads with a persistence that would embarrass an Irish setter. He must be dealt with firmly.

You must be joking.	*Vous rigolez.*	*Voo REE-goh-LAY.*
I never date the help.	*Je ne sors jamais avec le personnel.*	*Shuh nuh sore SHAM-ay ah-vek luh pair-son-el.*
Yes, I have a boyfriend.	*Oui, j'ai un copain.*	*WEE, shay uhn coh-pan.*
He's Sicilian.	*Il est sicilien.*	*Eel ay SEE-seel-yen.*
He likes to step on people's necks.	*Il aime bien piétiner la gueule des gens.*	*Eel em byen PYAY-tee-nay lah GULL day shon.*
I'm sure he'd be happy to break your legs.	*Je suis sûre qu'il serait heureux de vous casser les jambes.*	*Shuh swee SŸR keel ser-ay ur-UH duh voo CASS-ay lay shahmb.*

ACCOMMODATIONS

TINY HOTEL ROOMS OF FRANCE

A weak dollar can turn an already expensive French hotel room into a dramatically overpriced one. Coarse sheets, weird tubular pillows, and unidentifiable smells conspire to create a feeling of powerlessness in the tired or inexperienced traveler.

When this sort of emotion reaches the boiling point, it's time to begin complaining.

The bed is big enough for my leg.	*Le lit est assez grand pour ma jambe.*	*Luh LEE ay tass-ay GRON poor mah shahmb.*
The towel is big enough for my face.	*La serviette suffit tout juste à me sécher le visage.*	*Lah sair-vyet sÿ-FEE too JŸST ah muh SAY-shay luh vee-SAHJ.*
This is a room for a dwarf.	*C'est une chambre pour un nain.*	*Sait ÿn SHAHM-bruh poor uhn NAN.*
Every room is like this?	*Toutes les chambres sont comme ça?*	*TOOT lay shom-bruh sohn cum SAH?*
Are there so many dwarfs in France?	*Y a-t-il tant de nains en France?*	*Ee ah-teel TAHN duh nan on Fronce?*

THREATENING THE MAID

Maids are the same the world over. They want to get their work done before breakfast. But French people, and French maids in particular, feel morally superior to any person who is unconscious after 7:00 A.M. If you're still in bed at 9:00, honeymoon or no, expect no mercy. And show none.

Since maids don't expect tips, they rarely listen to reason; threats of bodily harm may be required.

Who's there?	*Qui est là?*	*Kee ay lah?*
Is there a fire?	*Il y a le feu?*	*Eel ee ah luh FUH?*
You just want to clean the room?	*Vous voulez seulement faire le ménage?*	*Voo voo-lay SUH-luh-mohn fair luh may-NAHJ?*
Could you come back after dawn?	*Revenez après le lever du soleil, voulez-vous?*	*RUH-vuh-nay ah-pray luh LUH-vay dÿ so-lay, voo-lay VOO?*
Please do not disturb me again.	*Ne me dérangez plus, s'il vous plaît.*	*Nuh muh DAY-rahn-shay PLŸ, seel voo play.*
Or I will scratch out your eyes.	*Ou je vous arrache les yeux.*	*Oo shuh vooz ah-RASH laze yuh.*

ACCOMMODATIONS

TIPPING

Bars and restaurants include a 15 percent *pourboire* (gratuity) in *l'addition* (the bill). This is frustrating for those who like to stiff waiters. However, customers who would like to be warmly welcomed upon their return to an establishment will leave an extra 5 or 10 percent tip, on top of the 15 percent already on the bill.

Most customers leave the coins they receive as change. The waiters then deposit these in their tip cups with the traditional sarcastic saying, *"Royale!"* which is supposed to reflect on a customer's generosity. It would never occur to a French waiter that a tip might reflect on the level of his service.

STIFFING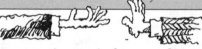

Theater ushers, even in movie houses, demand tips. Washroom attendants expect some coins but are somewhat less likely to scream if they don't get any. Denying such a person is sometimes possible with the right phrases.

In the theater:

| I insist. | J'insiste. | SHAHN-sees-tuh. |

Please let us find our own seats.	*Pourriez-vous nous laisser choisir nous-mêmes nos places?*	*POOR-ee-ay-VOO noo less-ay shwah-zeer noo-mem noh PLAHSS?*
I won't tip you.	*Votre pourboire passera à l'as.*	*Voh-truh poor-BWAR pass-er-AH ah lahss.*
Why don't you get a real job?	*Pourquoi ne cherchez-vous pas un vrai boulot?*	*Poor-KWAH nuh share-shay-voo PAH uhn VRAY boo-loh?*

In the washroom:

I didn't use any of your high-grade toilet paper.	*Je n'ai pas touché à votre papier hygiénique super-luxe.*	*Shuh nay PAH too-shay ah voh-truh PAH-pyay ee-jyen-eek SŸ-pair-lÿx.*
I didn't wash my hands.	*Je ne me suis pas lavé les mains.*	*Shuh nuh muh swee PAH lah-vay lay MAN.*
I didn't drip.	*Je n'ai pas laissé tomber une seule.*	*Shuh nay PAH less-ay TOM-bay ÿn sull.*
I don't owe you anything.	*Je ne vous dois pas un sou.*	*Shuh nuh voo dwah PAH uhn SOO.*

FASHION BONDAGE

The Parisian shopping experience is designed to make you feel even fatter and more slovenly than usual. The ensuing panic may cause you to buy more merchandise than you can possibly afford. The only way to avoid financial meltdown is to face the facts: No amount of spending can ever redeem you in the eyes of the slim, effortlessly attractive salepeople.

Oh look! It's the latest style from Madame Macbeth!	*Tiens! Le dernier style de Madame Macbeth!*	*Tyen! Luh dare-nyay STEEL duh Mah-dahm Mac-BET!*
It's sure to be fashionable for at least another fifteen minutes.	*Une mode qui en a encore pour un bon quart d'heure.*	*Ÿn mud key on ah on-KOOR poor uhn BUN car durr.*
This would look great.	*Cela aurait l'air extraordinaire.*	*Suh-lay aw-ray LARE ext-ROAR-dee-NAIR.*
On an alien.	*Sur un extra-terrestre.*	*Sÿr uhn extra-tair-ESS-truh.*
Maybe.	*Du moins, c'est possible.*	*Dÿ mwann, say pahss-EE-bluh.*

It reminds me of an Italian design I saw two years ago.	*Cela me fait penser à un modèle italien que j'ai vu il y a deux ans.*	*Suh-lah muh fay pon-say ah uhn moh-DELL ee-tal-YEN kuh shay vÿ eel ee ah duh ZON.*
Thank you, no. We're just looking.	*Non merci. Nous ne faisons que regarder.*	*Nohn mare-SEE. Noo nuh fay-zon kuh ruh-gar-DAY.*

DIETER'S DESIDERATA

Holy Saint Yves, Sacred Designer, Gifted Creator of *haute couture,* I beseech you to create just one of your heavenly dresses in my size. I have dieted like a jockey for seven years and still cannot fit into your latest creations, Your Blessed Femininity.

Très grand Saint-Yves, Dessinateur Sacré, Créateur Surdoué de la haute couture, je vous prie à genoux de créer pour moi un modèle divin que je puisse porter. Après sept longues années de régime de jockey, je n'arrive toujours pas à entrer dans vos dernières créations, Votre Féminité.

DEMON CHILDREN OF THE EIFFEL TOWER

There are thousands of talented pickpockets in Europe, and most of them are about four feet tall. They usually work in pairs and desist only upon threats of physical violence. Since most of us are reluctant to strike nine-year-old children, a few threatening phrases are supplied here.

Leave us alone.	*Fichez-nous la paix.*	*FEE-shay NOO lah pay.*
I bought a plastic Eiffel Tower yesterday.	*Hier, j'ai acheté une Tour Eiffel en plastique.*	*Ee-YAIR, shay ah-shuh-tay ÿn toor ay-FELL on PLAHSS-teek.*
I already own several kilos of brass jewelry.	*J'ai déjà plusieurs kilos de bijoux en alliage de laiton.*	*Shay day-SHAH PLY-zyur kee-loh duh BEE-shoo on ah-lee-yaj duh lay-TOHN.*
I haven't any coins.	*Je n'ai pas de petite monnaie.*	*Shuh nay PAH duh puh-teet moh-NAY.*
Back off.	*De l'air.*	*DUH lair.*
I'll break your neck, you little gypsy!	*Je te brise le cou, petit gitan!*	*Shuh tuh BREEZ luh coo, puh-tee shee-TAHN!*

Stop, thieves!	*Au voleur!*	*Oh voh-LURR!*
Police!	*Police!*	*Poh-LEASE!*
Arrest these children!	*Arrêtez ces enfants!*	*Ah-ray-TAY say zon-FON!*

PRAYER TO THE DON

Saint Carmine, Prince of Vengeance, Chief of
Vendettas, bring a horrible disease to the slimy
pickpocket who stole my wallet. In return, I
promise never to leave home again without
traveler's checks, Your Violence.

*Saint-Carmine, Prince de la Vengeance, Patron
des Vendettas, transmettez des maladies horribles
au pickpocket méprisable qui m'a délesté de mon
portefeuille. En reconnaissance de ça, je vous
promets de ne plus jamais quitter mon pays sans
des chèques de voyage, Votre Violence.*

THE MOST GIGANTIC ART MUSEUM ON EARTH

France has found favor with painters since Neanderthal times. Some of the greatest artists, Picasso and van Gogh among them, left their native lands and moved to France permanently.

Some historians believe that French sunlight has special qualities that bring colors to life for artists. Other experts insist that certain painters had simply bounced too many checks in their own countries.

Whatever the reason for their presence, artists have left millions of paintings and sculptures in France. You won't be able to avoid seeing some of them during your stay.

Which way to the Louvre?	*Quelle est la direction pour le Louvre?*	*Kel ay lah dee-reck-SYON poor luh LOO-vruh?*
Hey! The line starts back there.	*Eh! La queue commence là-bas.*	*EH! Lah KUH coh-monce lah bah.*
Who do you think you are? An Italian?	*Pour qui vous prenez-vous? Pour un macaroni?*	*Poor KEY voo pren-ay voo? Poor uhn mack-ah-roh-NEE?*

SIGHTS, SOUNDS, AND SMELLS

Is this the way to the *Mona Lisa*?	*La Joconde, c'est bien par là?*	*Lah shoh-COHN-duh, say byen par LAH?*
That's it? Just hanging on the wall like that?	*C'est tout? C'est celle qui pend au mur?*	*Say TOO? Say sell key pond oh mÿr?*
Where is the *Winged Victory*?	*Où est la Victoire de Samothrace?*	*OO ay lah veek-TWARR duh sah-moh-TRAHSS?*
She got kind of banged-up over the years, didn't she?	*Elle a pris un coup de vieux, vous ne trouvez pas?*	*El ah pree uhn coo duh VYUH, voo nuh troo-vay PAH?*
Pardon me, sir.	*Excusez-moi, monsieur.*	*Ex-KŸ-zay mwah, muh-SYUH.*
We have been here for four days and nights without food or water.	*Il y a quatre jours et quatre nuits que nous sommes ici sans nourriture ni la moindre goutte d'eau.*	*Eel ee ah KAT-ruh shoor ay KAT-ruh nÿ-ee kuh noo sum zee-SEE sahn noo-ree-TŸR nee lah MWAN-druh goot DOH.*
Could you be our guide to the exit?	*Pourriez-vous nous indiquer la sortie?*	*POOR-ee-ay-VOO noo ZAN-dee-KAY lah sore-TEE?*

INTELLIGENT COMMENTS ABOUT ART YOU CAN MAKE YOURSELF

Art museums have been ideal pickup spots for centuries, since they naturally screen out the unwashed, thereby ensuring that the pool of potential mates is held at a relatively high intellectual and social level.

But simply entering a house of worship such as the Louvre or Pompidou is not enough. Nor is "knowing what one likes" and gawking at it. One must *en mettre plein la vue* (sling bullshit) like Philippe de Montebello to be sure to impress one's fellow art lover and prospective victim.

Note: Do not attempt to pronounce van Gogh. It sounds something remotely like "van gohjgkhh." Stick with Vincent, "van-SAHN."

Notice how the fruit is dramatically outlined in black.	*Remarquez comme le fruit est souligné en noir d'une façon dramatique.*	*Ruh-mar-KAY cum luh frÿ-ee ay soo-lee-nyay on NWARR dÿn fah-son drah-mah-TEEK.*
Cézanne's little limes almost leap into your mouth.	*Les petits citrons verts de Cézanne vous sautent pratiquement dans la bouche.*	*Lay puh-tee see-tron VAIR duh Say-ZAHN voo sote prah-teek-mohn dahn lah BOOSH.*

Have you noticed Monet's bold use of blue here?	*Avez-vous remarqué l'audace du bleu dans ce Monet?*	*Ah-vay voo RUH-mar-KAY loh-DAHSS dÿ BLUH don suh Moh-NAY?*
The lone water lily signifies the essential loneliness of existence.	*Le nénuphar isolé incarne la solitude essentielle de l'existence.*	*Luh nay-nÿ-fahr ee-zoh-LAY een-carn lah SOLE-ee-TÿD ess-on-SYEL duh leg-zees-TONCE.*
But the water itself reminds us that passionate lovemaking helps us conquer that loneliness.	*Mais l'eau nous rappelle qu'un amour passionné nous aide à conquérir cette solitude.*	*May LOH noo rah-pell ken ah-MOOR pah-syon-ay noo-zed ah KON-kay-reer set SOLE-ee-TÿD.*
Let's talk about it over a cup of espresso.	*Parlons-en tout en prenant un café express.*	*PARL-on-zon toot on pruh-NON uhn KAH-fay ex-PRESS.*

NEGOTIATING THE TOPLESS BEACH

Attendants at French beaches will insist on payment. In exchange for one's hard-earned francs one may use a chair, an umbrella, and an outdoor shower. Changing rooms are also available, but the French are not *pudiques* (modest).

The attendant may shout and get red in the face when beach-goers refuse to buy any of his services, but there is no law against sitting on your own towel; beaches are public property.

What? I have to pay to sit here?	*Quoi? On doit payer pour s'asseoir ici?*	*Kwah? On dwah pay-YAY poor sass-warr ee-SEE?*
How much?	*Combien?*	*COHM-byen?*
Is it more to lie down?	*Et si on s'allonge, ça coûte plus cher?*	*Ay see on sall-ONSH, sah coot plÿ share?*
I refuse to pay you a cent. Leave me alone.	*Je refuse de vous payer un centime. Fichez-moi la paix.*	*Shuh ruh-fÿz duh voo pay-ay UHN sahn-teem. FEESH-ay mwah lah pay.*
Go ahead and call the cops, then.	*Allez-y, appelez les flics, alors.*	*AL-lay-zee, APP-lay lay fleek, ah-lore.*

Excuse me, miss, but I think you may be burning.	*Pardon mademoiselle, mais je crois que vous êtes en train de griller.*	*Par-DON mad-mwah-zel, may shuh KWAH kuh voo zet ohn TRAN duh gree-LAY.*
May I lend you some cocoa butter for those?	*Me permettez-vous de vous passez cette crème solaire pour ces deux-là?*	*Muh PAIR-met-ay VOO duh voo pahss-ay set crem so-lair poor say DUH-lah?*
You've had too much sun today.	*Vous êtes restée trop longtemps au soleil aujourd'hui.*	*Voo-zet rest-ay TROH lon-tahm oh so-LAY oh-shore-dwee.*
We must get you into a dark room immediately.	*On doit vous emmener dans une chambre noire immédiatement.*	*On dwah voo zom-mun-AY dahnz ÿn shahm-bruh NWARR ee-MAY-dyat-mohn.*
Yes. I'm a doctor.	*Oui. Je suis médecin.*	*WEE. Shuh swee MADE-san.*
Allow me to introduce myself.	*Permettez-moi de me présenter.*	*Pair-met-ay-MWAH duh muh PRAY-zon-tay.*

CULTIVATING YOUR ATTITUDE PROBLEM

Effective cursing in any language is a matter of attitude. However, the French have more "attitude" than any other species on earth.

When insulting one person, use the familiar *tu* rather than the formal *vous*. This implies condescension, which the French invented.

You bunch of camels!	*Bande de chameaux!*	*Bahn duh SHAM-oh!*
You peasants have truffles for brains!	*Vous les paysans, vous avez des truffes à la place de cerveau!*	*Voo lay pay-ee-ZOHN, vooz ah-vay day TRŸF ah lah plahss duh sair-VOH!*

You make me sick!	*Vous me rendez malade!*	*Voo muh RON-day mah-LAHD!*
Kiss my ass, you type of worthless pig!	*Je t'emmerde, espèce de porc à la manque!*	*Shuh tom-MAIRD, ess-pess duh PORE ah lah mahnk!*
I don't give a shit, defiler of virgins!	*Je n'en ai rien à foutre, espèce de dépuceleur de vierges.*	*Shuh non ay ryen ah FOO-truh, ess-pess duh DAY-pÿce-lur duh VYAIR-juh.*
Buzz off, depraved crab louse!	*Tire-toi, morpion!*	*Teer-TWAH, more-PYON!*
Boot-licker!	*Lèche-bottes!*	*LESH-butt!*
Up yours, dog-breath.	*Va te faire foutre, fumier à l'haleine de roquet.*	*VAH tuh fair FOO-truh, FÿY-myay ah lah-LENN duh roh-KAY.*
I'll see you in hell!	*On se reverra en enfer!*	*On suh ruh-vair-AH on non-fair!*
May the flames of Islam consume your degenerate life-style!	*Que les flammes de l'Islam consument votre train de vie dégénéré!*	*Kuh lay flom ·duh lease-LOM con-sÿm voh-trah tran duh VEE DAY-jen-air-ay!*

UNDERSTANDING EUROPEAN BUSINESS HOURS

Those who wonder why they so seldom see French people working may consult the guide below.

	What They're Doing	What's Happening to You
	MORNING	
8:00	Black coffee, lots of sugar. Looks like hot tar.	Attempt to sleep foiled by maid. Again.
9:00	Late for work. Coffee coursing through veins. Drive like mad.	Step out of hotel, almost killed by speeding motorist.
10:00	Chat on phone. Quasi-business purpose for conversation.	Try to change money, but mob overwhelms lone clerk.
11:00	Make lunch plans.	Shopkeeper on phone. Fail to get his attention.
	AFTERNOON	
12:00	Drop by a friend's office.	Attempt to contact local travel agent. She isn't in.
1:00	Late for lunch. Drive like hell.	Ride in taxi, almost killed on way to museum.

🏛 BUREAUCRACY AND CULTURE

2:00	Lunch with entire family.	Museum closed.
3:00	Speak with friends on telephone, plan evening.	Begin drinking.
4:00	More coffee.	Return to bank. Ready to kill line jumpers.

EVENING		
5:00	Average 180 kph on drive to office.	Huge crowd at travel agency. Chuckle good-naturedly.
6:00	Look up from phone call. Make hand motion: *"Un moment."*	Obtain francs and tickets. Finally. Head back to café.
7:00	Race home. Change clothes. Argue with spouse/children.	Seated in café, almost killed by speeding car.
8:00	Race to meet lover. Almost killed by speeding vehicle.	Decide to "borrow" big Citroën. Go for joyride.
10:00	Quiet dinner at home.	At dinner, restaurant seems full of grotesque tourists.

LATE EVENING		
12:00	Retire to separate bedroom.	Unable to find taxi.
1:00	Well-earned sleep.	Eventually find hotel. Greet maids beginning their day's work.

BUREAUCRACY AND CULTURE 🏛

WAITING FOR GODOT'S TELEGRAM

Many French people rely on the post office (PTT) for telephones, telegrams, even checking accounts. One can find stamps at the PTT, of course, but these are for sale in cafés and tobacco shops as well. Postal workers are not known for being helpful; you'll get more sympathy from barracuda.

The French will loudly defend their postal service as being far superior to the American version. That, of course, isn't much of a boast.

I would like to send this airmail to California.	*Je voudrais envoyer cette lettre par avion en Californie.*	*Shuh voo-DRAY on-vwah-YAY set LET-ruh par ah-VYON on cal-ee-for-NEE.*
How much will that cost?	*Combien cela va-t-il me coûter?*	*Com-BYEN suh-lah vah-teel muh COO-tay?*
Look at all your record books! How quaint.	*Regardez tous ces livres! Comme vous êtes vieux jeu.*	*RUH-gar-DAY too say LEE-vruh! Cum voo zet vyuh shuh.*
Do you think it will arrive in time for Christmas?	*Pensez-vous que la lettre arrivera à temps pour Noël?*	*PONCE-ay voo kuh lah LET-ruh ah-REEV-uh-rah ah tohmp poor noh-EL?*

🏛 *BUREAUCRACY AND CULTURE*

No? In time for Easter, then?	*Non? Pour Pâques, alors?*	Nohn? Poor PAK, ah-LORE?
Maybe his/her great-grand-children will live to receive it.	*Peut-être ses arrières-petits-enfants la recevront-ils avant de mourir de vieillesse.*	Puh-TET-ruh saze AR-ee-YAIR puh-teez on-FON lah RUH-suh-vron-TEEL ah-VONT duh moo-REER duh vyay-ESS.
No need to apologize.	*Ne vous excusez pas.*	Nuh vooz ex-CŸ-zay pah.
Thank you for being so gracious.	*Merci de votre amabilité.*	Mare-SEE duh voh-truh AM-ah-bee-lee-tay.
Have you been checked for rabies recently?	*Est-ce-que vous avez été exam-iné pour la rage récemment?*	Ess-kuh vooz ah-vay ay-tay ex-am-ee-nay poor lah RAHJ ray-sah-mahn?
Excuse me, but have you a porcupine stuck up your rear end?	*Pardonnez-moi, mais avez-vous un porc-épic coincé entre les fesses?*	PAR-don-ay-mwah, may ah-vay-voo uhn PORK-ay-pick kwan-say on-truh lay FESS?
Same to you and your grandmother.	*La même chose à vous et à votre grand-mère.*	Lah mem shose ah VOO ay ah voh-truh gron-MAIR.

WINE AND FOOD

NO BAD WAITERS

Many restaurant employees, from *saucier* to *sommelier,* bear emotional scars from past experiences serving foreigners. Once they hear you speaking English, they cannot help but assume that you are a Stone Age pagan. When a waiter is suffering from such a prejudice, his manners may slip to reveal the beast beneath the tuxedo. Below are a few phrases that should keep him in form, or at least allow you to hold your own.

Sir, is it true that you're ashamed of your menu?	*Monsieur, est-ce vrai que vous avez honte de votre menu?*	*Muh-SYUH, ess VRAY kuh vooz ah-vay ONT duh voh-truh men-Ÿ?*
Perhaps you would show us a copy, then.	*Pourriez-vous nous en faire voir un exemplaire, alors.*	*Poor-ee-ay voo noo-zon fare VWARR uhn ex-ohm-plair, ah-LORE.*
Could we have a pitcher of water?	*Pourrait-on avoir une carafe d'eau?*	*Poo-rate-on ah-VWARR ÿn kah-rahf DOH?*
Tap water, please. With ice.	*De l'eau du robinet, s'il vous plaît. Avec des glaçons.*	*Duh loh dÿ ROH-bee-nay, seel voo play. Ah-vek day GLAH-son.*

It's the hard, cold stuff the Eskimos like so much.	*Ce truc dur et froid que les Esquimaux aiment tellement.*	*Suh trÿk DŸR ay FWAH kuh laze ESS-kee-moh EM tel-luh-mahn.*
If you continue to take that attitude, I swear I'll smother my soufflé in ketchup.	*Si vous continuez à vous conduire comme ça, je jure de noyer mon soufflé dans du ketchup.*	*See voo con-tin-ÿ-ay ah voo con-DWEER cum sah, shuh SHOOR duh NWAH-yay mohn soo-FLAY don dÿ ket-SHUP.*
I'm afraid it's now past dinnertime.	*J'ai bien peur que l'heure du dîner ne soit passée.*	*Shay byen PUR kuh LUR dÿ dee-NAY nuh swah POSS-ay.*
Please change my order to a Continental breakfast.	*Veuillez changer ma commande pour un petit déjeuner à la française.*	*Vuh-yay SHON-shay mah com-MAHND poor uhn puh-TEE day-shuh-nay ah lah fron-SEZ.*
Wake me when it arrives.	*Réveillez-moi quand il arrivera.*	*RUH-vay-ay mwah con teel ah-REE-vuh-rah.*

ORGANS YOU MAY WISH TO AVOID EATING

The French are very resourceful when it comes to consuming animal parts. Travelers who prefer to remain unfamiliar with the appearance, texture, and flavor of these dishes may need these excuses to turn down the waiter's unwelcome suggestions.

I had blackbird pie for lunch.	*J'ai mangé du pâté de merle pour le déjeuner.*	*Shay MON-shay dÿ PAT-ay duh MAIRL poor luh DAY-shun-ay.*
I'm trying to cut down on liver from anemic newborn calves.	*J'essaie de restreindre ma consommation de foie de veau.*	*Shess-ay duh ress-tran-druh mah con-som-ah-SYON duh FWAH duh voh.*
I'm allergic to calf's marrow soup.	*Je suis allergique au potage à la moelle de veau.*	*Shuh swee ZAL-air-jeek oh POH-tahj ah lah MWAHL duh voh.*
I don't think thyroid glands would go well with my appetizer.	*Je ne pense pas que les ris de veau se marient bien avec mon hors-d'oeuvre.*	*Shuh nuh ponce pah kuh luh REE duh voh suh MAH-ree byen ah-VEK mohn or-DUH-vruh.*

✕ WINE AND FOOD

Pig's blood sausage is just too rich for me.	*Le boudin noir est un peu trop lourd à mon goût.*	*Luh boo-dan NWAR ay tuhn puh troh LOOR ah mohn goo*
I believe a stew of goose organs and goose blood is out of season.	*Je ne pense pas que ce soit la saison pour du civet de tripes d'oie au sang.*	*Shuh ne ponce pah kuh suh swah lah SAY-zohn poor dÿ SEE-vay duh TREEP dwah oh sohn.*
I'm saving stew of blood-sucking eels for a very special occasion.	*Je réserve la lamproie à la bordelaise pour une occasion spéciale.*	*Shuh ray-zerv lah lom-pwah ah lah bord-uh-LEZ poor ÿn oh-caz-yohn SPAY-syal.*
Tonight I'm in the mood for filet of sole with French fries.	*Ce soir j'ai envie d'un filet de sole avec des frites.*	*Suh SWAR shay on-vee duhn FEE-lay duh SOLE ah-vek day FREET.*

WINE AND FOOD

WINE TALK OF THE SOPHISTICATES

Of all the products of
France, wine is one of the
most admired by French-
men and foreigners alike.
Talking knowledgeably
about wine marks the
true sophisticate.

The wine has great legs.	*Ce vin a de la jambe.*	*Suh VAN ah duh lah shom-buh.*
Yes, but its buttocks are wrinkled.	*Oui, mais il a la fesse fripée.*	*WEE, may eel ah lah FESS free-pay.*
The Haut-Médoc tries to grease the palate but scratches instead.	*Ce Haut-Médoc essaie de me graisser le palais mais n'arrive qu'à l'écorcher.*	*Suh OH-may-DUK ESS-ay duh muh GRESS-ay luh pah-LAY may nah-reev kah LAY-cor-shay.*
This Beaucastel rouge is plump and amusing.	*Ce Beaucastel rouge est calin et bien charnu.*	*Suh BOH-cass-tel roo jhay CAH-lan ay BYEN shar-nÿ.*
What a delightful aroma of hazelnuts and sardines!	*Quel superbe bouquet de noisettes et de sardines!*	*Kell sÿ-PAIR-buh bouquet duh NWAH-zet ay duh sar-DEEN!*

🍴 WINE AND FOOD

The Armagnac was clever but shy.	*L'Armagnac était futé mais trop discret.*	*LAR-mah-nyak ay-tay foo-TAY may TROH dees-cray.*
The Vouvray is pimply but forthright.	*Le Vouvray a des aspérités mais il est sincère.*	*Luh voo-VRAY ah day ZAH-spare-ee-tay may eel AY san-sair.*
The Château Montrose is an ungrateful bitch.	*Le Château Montrose est une roulure sans gratitude.*	*Luh SHA-toh mohn-rose ay tÿn roo-LŸR sohn grah-tee-TŸD.*

This Sauternes has socialist tendencies.	*Ce Sauternes a des tendances socialistes.*	*Suh Saw-TAIRN ah day ton-DONCE soh-syah-leest.*
Romanée-Conti is forever a sublime ferret in my underpants.	*Le Romanée-Conti restera à jamais un sublime rat de cave dans mon caleçon.*	*Luh ROH-mah-nay cohn-TEE rest-uh-rah ah shah-may uhn sÿ-bleem RAH duh cahv dahn mohn CAL-sohn.*

DOMINATING THE DISCO

French people like to go to the disco. The trouble is, they can't dance. Because they are about as funky as the Japanese, the French love to watch Americans go wild. This is one of the two things Frenchmen admire about the United States.

The other is California.

I learned to dance in L.A.	*J'ai appris à danser à Los Angeles.*	*Shay ah-PREE ah DON-say ah loss AN-jeh-less.*
I live in San Francisco.	*J'habite à San Francisco.*	*Shah-BEET ah SAHN Frahn-see-skoh.*
Marin County, actually. You know California?	*Le Marin County, en fait. Vous connaissez la Californie?*	*Luh MAH-ran con-TEE, on fet. Voo con-ay-SAY lah cal-ee-for-NEE?*
Of course, I have a house in Malibu as well.	*Bien sûr, j'ai également une maison à Malibu.*	*Byen SŸR, shay ay-gal-MAHN ÿn may-ZOHN ah mal-ee-BOO.*
Sometimes I need to be near my movie studios.	*J'ai parfois besoin d'être près de mes studios de cinéma.*	*Shay par-FWAH buzz-WAN det-ruh PRAY duh may stÿ-dyoh duh see-nay-MAH.*

🕺 *CAFE AND NIGHTLIFE*

Aren't you an actor/actress?	*Vous êtes acteur/actrice?*	*Voo-zet ak-TUR/ ak-TREECE?*
You really should have a screen test.	*Vous devriez vraiment faire un essai à l'écran.*	*Voo dev-ree-ay VRAY-mahn fair uhn ess-ay ah lay-CRAHN.*
This evening, perhaps?	*Ce soir, peut-être?*	*Suh SWARR, puh tet-ruh?*
Let's split, babe.	*On se tire, poupée.*	*On suh TEER, poo-pay.*

EXOTIC DRINKS OF THE FRENCH NIGHTCLUB

Once they leave the dinner table, the French seem to forget about their *vins* and *apéritifs,* undoubtedly the finest in the world. By the time nightclubbers reach their destination, they seem to have only one thing in mind: getting ripped.

One needs four words to encompass a French disco's entire beverage selection: scotch, vodka, Coke (*koh-KAH*), and Banga (*ban-GAH*), a type of orange soda. These can be drunk in any combination without offending anyone.

CAFE AND NIGHTLIFE

CAFE ETIQUETTE

No matter how drunk you get:
▶ Do not sing, even if you suddenly realize how to speak French.
▶ Do not make political speeches or announcements.
▶ Do not slap strangers on the back.
▶ Do not force-feed *apéritifs to* strangers or their dogs.

EXISTENTIALISM AND OTHER BULL

France has produced many important philosophers for two reasons: (1) the French love to sit in cafés and say things; and (2) saying intelligent things is the best way to seduce innocent young graduate students.

To continue the tradition of these innovative playboys, travelers should sprinkle their conversation with the following classics.

René Descartes:

I think in French; therefore I am.	*Je pense en français; donc je suis.*	*Shuh ponce on fron-SAY; donk shuh swee.*
I think; therefore I am French.	*Je pense; donc je suis français.*	*Shuh ponce; donk shuh swee fron-SAY.*

CAFE AND NIGHTLIFE

Fred Kierkegaard:

The less I think, the more I am.	*Moins je pense, plus j'existe.*	*Mwann shuh ponce, plÿ SHEG-zeest.*
Passion is the hallmark of existence, my little cabbage.	*La passion est la garantie de l'existence, mon petit chou.*	*Lah PASS-yon ay lah GARE-ahn-TEE duh LEGG-zeest-AHNCE, mon puh-TEE shoe.*

Jean-Paul Sartre:

I hate people who say they are existentialists.	*Je haïs les gens qui se disent existentialistes.*	*Shuh hay-ee lay shon key suh DEEZ EGG-zee-STON-shal-EAST.*

Jacques Cousteau:

Zuh most graceful creatures can also be zuh deadliest.	*Les créatures les plus gracieuses peuvent être aussi les plus mortelles.*	*Lay CRAY-ah-ture lay plÿ GRAH-see-YUZ puhv ET-ruh oh-SEE lay plÿ more-TELL.*
In zuh sea, zaire ees no cruelty, only zuh struggle to survive.	*Dans la mer il n'y a pas de cruauté, mais seulement l'angoisse de survivre.*	*Dahn lah maire eel nyah pah duh CRŸ-oh-TAY, may suh-luh-mahn lang-WASS duh sÿr-VEEV-ruh.*

CAFE AND NIGHTLIFE

BANISHING SHRIMPS

Frenchmen are often less robust than their American counterparts. Their *savoir-faire* tends to make up for it; their accents alone are enough to make many American women melt. But women who'd like to hold out for somebody at least an inch taller than they are will need a few killing phrases to get rid of diminutive hangers-on.

Excuse me. I didn't see you down there.	*Oh pardon. Je ne vous avais pas vu là, tout en bas.*	*Oh PAR-dohn. Shuh nuh voo zah-vay pah VŸ lah, TOO tohn bah.*
Stand up!	*Debout!*	*DUH-boo!*
Have you lost your mommy?	*Tu as perdu ta maman?*	*Tÿ ah pair-DŸ tah mah-mahn?*
Let me guess. You're a jockey, right?	*Attendez un peu. Vous êtes jockey, hein?*	*AT-on-day uhn puh. Voo-zett show-KAY, ehn?*
No! Wait! You're a movie star!	*Non! J'y suis! Vous êtes une vedette de cinéma.*	*Nohn! SHEE swee! Voo zet ÿn VUH-dett duh see-nay-MAH.*
You played alongside Snow White, right?	*Vous avez joué dans Blanche Neige, pas vrai?*	*Voo zah-vay shew-ay dohn blonsh-NEHJ, pah VRAY?*

Women must love you.	*Je suis sûr que les femmes vous adorent.*	*Shuh swee SŸR kuh lay fahm voo ZAH-door.*
At least those who like to have their kneecaps licked.	*Enfin, celles qui aiment se faire bouffer les rotules.*	*On-FANN, sell kee em suh fair BOO-fay lay roh-tÿl.*

FAVORITE PET NAMES

The following French terms of endearment are authentic. It is better to use them than to translate your personal favorites. "My sweet potato pie," for example, doesn't work. Yams are not widely admired in France.

My cabbage.	*Mon chou.*	*Mohn shoe.*
My chicken.	*Ma poulette/mon poulet.*	*Mah POO-lett/ mohn POO-lay.*
My little doe/big buck.	*Ma bichette/mon grand bichou.*	*Mah bee-SHET/ mohn gron bee-SHOE.*
My hen.	*Ma cocotte.*	*Mah coh-CUT.*
My dove.	*Ma tourterelle.*	*Mah TOOR-tuh-rell.*
My kitten.	*Mon minet.*	*Mohn MEE-nay.*
My flea.	*Ma puce.*	*Mah pÿs.*

CAFE AND NIGHTLIFE

THE WORDS OF LOVE

Any man hoping to offer serious romantic competition in Europe must exaggerate. There is a certain inflation inherent in French "lines" because they've been in use for thousands of years.

Phrases we consider original and cunning, such as "What a pretty name," and "Do you come here often?" lost their power back in the thirteenth century.

You are one fabulous babe.	*Vous êtes une super nana.*	*Voo zet ÿn SOO-pair nah-nah.*
You are an angel come to earth.	*Vous êtes un ange descendu sur terre.*	*Voo zet uh NONJ day-sohn-DŸ sÿr tair.*
Your eyes are as blue as the sea of my love for you is large.	*Vos yeux sont aussi bleus que l'océan de mon amour pour vous est grand.*	*Voh zyuh sohn toh-see BLUH kuh LOH-say-ahn duh mohn ah-MOOR poor voo ay grahn.*
I don't care if the sun never rises again, so long as you love me.	*Cela m'est bien égal que le soleil ne se lève plus, si seulement vous m'aimez.*	*Suh-lah may byen nay-GAL kuh luh so-LAY nuh suh lev plÿ, see suh-luh-mohn voo MAY-may.*

I am only an earthworm without you.	*Sans vous je ne suis qu'un ver de terre.*	*Sahn VOO shuh nuh swee kuhn VAIR duh tair.*
Come away with me on my yacht, my little cabbage.	*Enfuyons nous ensemble sur mon yacht, mon petit chou.*	*ON-fwee-yon noo on-SOM-bluh sÿr mon YUT, mohn puh-tee SHOE.*
And what is your name, my jewel of thirty-six carats?	*Comment vous appelez-vous, mon bijou de trente-six carats?*	*COM-on voo ZAP-lay voo, mohn BEE-shoo duh tron-SEECE cah-rah?*
Ah! Your husband!/My wife!	*Ciel! Votre mari!/Ma femme!*	*See-YELL! Voh-truh MAH-ree!/ Mah FAHM!*
Au revoir.	*Au revoir.*	*Oh ruh-VWARR.*

CAFE AND NIGHTLIFE

YOUR EMERGENCY CONFESSION

When far from home, some people do things they later regret. Luckily for them, France is still a Catholic country. The French see no need to live with their guilt; they simply confess. For those who wish to engage in this clever practice, the following phrases may be helpful.

Forgive me, Father, for I have sinned.	*Pardonnez-moi, mon Père, car j'ai péché.*	*PAR-donn-ay-MWAH, mohn PAIR, car shay PAY-shay.*
It has been six hours/days/ weeks/months/ years since my last confession.	*Cela fait six heures/jours/ semaines/mois/ ans que je ne me suis pas confessé(e).*	*Suh-lah fay SEE zuhr/shoor/suh-MEN/mwah/on kuh shuh nuh muh swee pah CON-fay-say.*
I picked up a girl/boy in a fine restaurant.	*J'ai dragué une fille/un garçon dans un restaurant vraiment bien.*	*Shay DRAH-gay ÿn fee/uhn gar-SOHN dahn zuhn res-toh-rohn VRAY-mahn byen.*
Yes, I realize how serious that is.	*Oui, oui, je sais que c'est très grave.*	*Wee, wee, shuh SAY kuh say tray grahv.*

But I also drank a Gewürztztraminer with roasted duck.	*Mais j'ai bu aussi du Gewürztztraminer avec du canard rôti.*	*May shay bÿ oh-SEE dÿ guh-VAIRTS-trah-MEAN-er ah-vek dÿ can-ARR roh-TEE.*
Are you choking, Father?	*Vous suffoquez, mon Père?*	*Voo sÿ-foh-KAY, mohn pair?*
Wait, there's more. I made love to a Belgian.	*Attendez, ce n'est pas tout. J'ai couché avec un/une belge.*	*Ah-TOHN-day, suh NAY pah too. Shay coo-SHAY ah-vek uhn/ÿn belge.*
Burning at the stake does seem a little severe.	*Brûler au bûcher me semble un peu dur.*	*Brÿ-lay oh BÿShay muh somm-bluh uhn puh DÿR.*
How about a few thousand "Our Fathers" instead?	*Que pensez-vous de quelques milliers de "Notre Père"?*	*Kuh PONN-say voo duh kell-kuh mee-lee-yay duh noh-truh PAIR?*
Thank you, Father. Oh, one more thing.	*Merci, mon Père. Oh, un moment.*	*Mare-SEE, mohn pair. Oh, uhn moh-MOHN.*
Can you recommend a good restaurant?	*Vous ne connaîtriez pas un bon petit restaurant?*	*Voo nuh con-ay-tree-ay PAH uhn bohn puh-tee res-toh-ROHN?*

THE MODEL GUEST 🧳

YOUR FIRST RURAL EXPERIENCE

Every year, a few lucky people get the chance to stay on a farm with a French family. They should be ready for hard work and delicious home-cooked meals. Getting along with the family should be no problem if you memorize a few key phrases.

I'm afraid I don't know much about milking/ slaughtering cows.	*Je crains ne pas bien m'y connaître dans la traite des vaches/ l'abattage du bétail.*	*Shuh cran nuh pah mee con-ET-ruh dahn lah tret day vahsh/lah-bah-TASH dÿ bay-TIE.*
You mean you shovel this much every day?	*Vous voulez dire que vous bêchez tout ça chaque jour?*	*Voo voo-lay DEER kuh voo bay-shay too sah shack SHOOR?*
You mean we're going to kill this little calf? In honor of my visit?	*Vous voulez dire qu'on va tuer ce petit veau? En mon honneur?*	*Voo voo-lay DEER kohn vah TŸ-ay suh puh-tee VOH? On mohn noh-NUR?*
Actually, I prefer my veal on the hoof.	*Pour tout vous avouer, je préfère le veau sur pied.*	*Poor too voo zah-voo-AY, shuh pray-FAIR luh VOH sÿr PYAY.*

THE INEVITABLE THANK-YOU LETTER

Experienced travelers always write *un billet de remerciments* (a thank-you note) to a kind host or hostess, and a postcard or two to each interesting person they have met on a trip. This ensures a warm welcome upon return to France, and often leads to kind invitations, the sort that can help one avoid those bothersome restaurant and hotel bills. The following are a few common phrases used in letter writing.

Dear Pierre/Dear Monique,	*Cher Pierre/Chère Monique,*
Thank you for the unforgettable day/evening/ weekend.	*Je tiens à vous remercier pour cette journée/cette soireé/ce week-end inoubliable.*
I'll never see Paris the same way again.	*Je ne verrai plus jamais Paris avec les mêmes yeux.*
You've opened up a whole new world for me.	*Vous m'avez fait découvrir un monde entièrement nouveau.*
I've got a terrible rash that won't go away.	*J'ai attrapé une urticaire dont je n'arrive pas à me guérir.*

THE MODEL GUEST 🧳

But I must say your cooking was magnificent.	*Mais je dois reconnaître que votre cuisine était superbe.*
The carbon duck was particularly fine.	*Le canard calciné était vraiment extraordinaire.*
As was the sly, aggressive Margaux.	*De même que le Margaux, astringent et un peu traître.*
The "dessert" you had planned was also delicious.	*Le "dessert" que vous aviez prévu était également délicieux.*
My only regret is that it was all over so quickly.	*Mon seul regret est d'en avoir à peine vu la couleur.*
I look forward to seeing you again someday.	*J'espère avoir le plaisir de vous revoir un jour.*
Perhaps by then one of us will be divorced/bilingual.	*Peut-être qu'à ce moment là, l'un de nous deux sera-t-il divorcé/bilingue.*
Hope your rash is every bit as virulent as mine.	*J'espère que votre éruption est aussi virulente que la mienne.*
Yours truly, (Your name)	*Veuillez agréer l'assurance de mon souvenir ému, (Your name)*